JAMES
KOLLER
CALIFORNIA
POEMS

4/71
3.00
(15.00 Cloth)

by James Koller

Two Hands, Poems 1959-61 (1965)
Brainard & Washington Street Poems (1965)
The Dogs & Other Dark Woods (1966)
Some Cows, Poems of Civilization & Domestic Life (1966)
I Went To See My True Love (1967)

JAMES
KOLLER
CALIFORNIA
POEMS

BLACK SPARROW PRESS

LOS ANGELES   1971

Some of these poems appeared first in the following periodicals: *Audit/East West; Hotcha* (Zurich); *Intransit; Nexus; Out of Sight; The Paris Review; Quixote; Stony Brook; The Wivenhoe Park Review; The World.*

Black Sparrow Press
P.O. Box 25603
Los Angeles, California
90025

SBN 87685-092-1 (paper)
87685-093-X (signed cloth)

CALIFORNIA POEMS / I

"That fall, on bicycle"
HOW IT HAPPENED
RADIO POEM
WISH YOU WERE HERE!!
HERE I AM AGAIN
I'M GOING HOME!
"I ain't no Shanshiro Sugata"
"So early to wake"
"the blackberries were not ripe"
POEM FOR YELLOW HAIR
"BLUE GREEN A MOUNTAIN LAKE THE SKY"
"I'D CLIMB THE HIGHEST MOUNTAIN WITH YOU"
" ' SORRY LADY, THE TRAIN JUST LEFT 10 MINUTES AGO' "
I WENT TO SEE MY TRUE LOVE
"I tried to write you a song"
"born at night"
THE DREAM YOU TOLD
SNOW ON MT. ST. HELENA

SPARKES ROAD
CALIFORNIA POEMS / II

"We change to keep all else the same"
"Crossed & crossed the barbed stems"
"I was crawling around on the floor with her sister"
"Venus, pink, over the trees"
"Mars, opalescent orange, McIbbon's crystal ball"
"I crawled over the dark ground"
"the deer, out of the trees, downhill"
"lightning, coming home"
"we came out of that city"
"*All through the night they rode*"

CALIFORNIA POEMS / I

That fall, on bicycle, at dusk, I heard the Canadian Geese—
honking, low over the Samish, out the mouth
south, after the sun

    && winter was early & hard

driving to Bothell, the seminary lawn
covered with coots

    my daughter woke me with a flute

off San Rafael Creek, the bay—today—full of coots

    I saw a girl in Burlington
    with a wild goose
    blazoned on the back of her jacket

    she was going to the bowling alley

I was driving my truck home from the dump

ARE YOU HUNGRY?   ARE YOU HUNGRY?

    don't feed the bears

I had roses in my hat—inside
three of them, a rose for each
& I gave them all to you

        a branch of roses
        her hair & the branch
        her arms & legs
        the white dress in half light

        in the cherry tree
        we reached into the limbs
        ate in the dark

        the bears prowling
        a couple
        in the front seat of the pink mercury

I can't find your tucking combs
      it ain't important
they were here a minute ago
      so were you

        dead, I thought
        you didn't move, she said
        when I covered you

        on the prod, prowl

        with a big stick

            (bear with me)

hungry, feed them, in the beginning
before any further conversation
any introduction—

three roses.   Out of my head

I dreamed I went with you

I dreamed I took you

where were you
I was there, saw you
looking for you
I was there, where you found me

What a way to go.

Cindy's got religion, she never had it before.

around a fire—guitars, tin dishes, crickets & mosquitos
smoke

we were higher up—above the timber

your hair, your hands

Jack Daniels, I love you of old
you rob my poor pockets

made me sicker than sick

maybe my heart wasn't in it

of course it was

one rose for one pair of lips
tight in her teeth
the stem green

ARE YOU HUNGRY?

STILL?

    I did take you. It was a great trip,
    remind me to tell you of it—

I am burning the candle on one end

CLOSE THE DOORS, THE BEARS ARE COMING!!!
Aren't you going to close the doors???

    one for each of the original states

     only they were in a circle

   which is the only place to be

         *

     one rose, I'm
   still hungry

         *

sky rockets exploding, Thomas The Dog
   looking out the window

the whistles die in the dark, July 4th

      yankee doodle dandy
      stuck my doodle in a dandy
      pulled it out & called it
      done

RADIO POEM

Wiggle Yr Toes Chew

(Eve, of Destruction)

somebody else singing yr song, again

contemplation

falling stars

WHOOSH BOOM

Hey, Red! Yeah, yeah. Ride.

Going my way?

Hey, Red, yeah—wiggle

someone to know me
someone to throw me

EEHAA!!!

choose yr partner, split lady split
wiggle chew

WHOOSH BANG!!!!!

(I'll be here. Don't ask why.
Won't tell anybody.
My feelings are hurt.
Sonumbitch.)

show me the valley—show me the trail

(devastation)

You & I. Merry-go-round
all yoops loops the loops
       HOOPLA!!!

((A Public Service Message:

       whatever it is you have in yr mouth—))

everybody is singing yr song

                    (NEWS! NEWS! THE ANTS
                    are in yr underwear.

                         what are they after?

                              come, come)

whatever, whatever

            raw red frayed tongue yr hands
            ain't making
            any headway

"Baby, Laugh At Me, & I'll Cry For You"

WISH YOU WERE HERE!!

whatcha doing?
running around much?

      (heard from your sister lately?)

        you'll notice I asked that
          quietly

YOU!!!
      (was that you or me?)

&c.

like I said, like

      I have missed you

  (we should've gone when we had the chance
  we should've—I still see your hand
  tracing unknown figures on the car seat
     between us)

I read a lot into doorways, partings
  like when we talked about being

      AVAILABLE

      NOT back there, you ain't

            the gal
    who made a fool out of me?

I didn't realize—

& on & on
where she stops nobody knows

                    (the odds are
                    against me)

I am sitting in the kitchen, drinking wine
white wine, a green cup, the table brown
        THE RADIO IS ON:
                        "Why do you say that?"
                        "Music is the language of love!"

NUFF SAID?

miss you (wasn't
enough)
            "sad the shape I'm in"

((Eighteen inches of snow in Whitefish.
  Two buddies & myself
  once spent hours in Whitefish, looking
  for gas—picked up two gals
  who showed us a lake near town
  before they showed us to the gas station.

  I was 18
  & lonely))

freedom flashing

                    like a white fish

            what are the odds?

        where are we stranded??

        (all the roads between us
            closed)

(16)

still drinking my breakfast tea
while the police make merry
chasing cars up & down
this hill
        tonight

they hardly notice me
by candlelight, scratching
in small tight script

I MUST LOOSEN UP—TELL ALL

I thought I heard three taps on the window
turned off all the lights—nobody there
   that I could see   & I keep hoping

  that somehow, you'd

     (by candlelight!? no violins!?!)

my cigar stinks in the ashtray
my tea cold since morning

            I'm thinking
of another wanderer come home
wishing I was in your bed
filling you with some strange tale

it wasn't you
who the hell was it
    (I close all the windows, pull the shades
    nobody can see me

       I can't see them, either)

THIS AIN'T THE NIGHT FOR LOVE * QUIT IT

Do you want an apple?
I'll take off my shoes.

I'M GOING HOME!

                you forgot
your raincoat
I'm bringing it, I'm
coming home

        leave my potatoes, oranges
        toilet paper & peanuts

  (I haven't shit in the woods since 56—Smith
  a roll of toilet paper, a red flag, in hand)

going home, the rain

        so hard the wipers shorted out,
        the horn stuck, the ignition wouldn't turn off

        piss on a flat rock

                when god was a little boy

                        a gray squirrel
                top of a fencepost

        leave one rifle, 16 shells, 2 maps
                the rifle a Remington, bolt, 30-06
                the shells Winchester, same caliber
                the maps, Liberty & Mt. Stuart, 15', 1961

                        a nuthatch nearly lit on my shoulder
                        another on the gun barrel

                        he had a green bill

                coming down, off Shuksan

(18)

dark, alone
I almost shot a porcupine

thought he was a bear

(Sandy Dances in Eugene, white fringe
Louie Louie, If I Had A Hammer)

you win, you win

see you another day

going home

the rings are chrome
if they don't seat by 5,000
complain

"this ain't no original"

we ate lunch
Someplace
a dead salmon
awash at our feet

the white pup, like a Samoyed
want to buy him?
took him in trade, thought
I could sell him

cars people on foot, Snoqualmie Pass
the mountain goat like a patch of leftover snow

oak for heat
fir for kindling, cooking

"those are leaves burning"

the girl in the laundromat, Seattle

black net stockings
a hole just below her left knee

the leaves falling, blowing away
we walked the early morning streets
empty except for us &
the giant orange streetcleaners

(David or Andrew, Rebecca Ann
who you gonna be, Smith baby?)

hail in with the rain

in Eugene, drove the wrong way down a one-way
the officer, when he saw California plates
Washington driver's license

Where DO you live??

I'M *GOING* HOME

you win you win

"every time you come, I get pains in my belly"

gas
Wolf Creek, Weed, & Maxwell

How's Thomas?
Fine.
How do you know?
I'm here with him.

Hang on, Sloopy.

"Well, if it ain't old Wolf Tit"

I ain't no Shanshiro Sugata
   smiling in my sleep—
the crazy one taking his knife from my throat
   chewing his nails in fear

           "I'm in on something—
              this ain't no one night stand"

        but my eyes are open

why do you walk so fast?

   a lope
      (can't walk a straight line
          unless I walk fast)

   the secret is out

"It is a heavy load—
    they all are"

        put in hot water, a toilet
           Kyoto, settling in

              an old roommate returning

I bought another bottle
(visitors from the north)
Inventory: 1 gallon red wine—Paisano
            11 12 oz. bottles of beer—Budweiser
            1/5 gallon sake—Koshu
            1/5 gallon bourbon—Jack Daniels
            1/5 gallon rye—Old Overholt
(Ed & Carole, Vanny, Paula, Nico & Philip)
        settling in

& tea: Darjeeling, Lapsang Suchong, Oolong, Gen-mai

(21)

all cups full

the wolf looks after his family

I'm looking

wind warnings in the Siskiyou
snow down to 2,000 feet in the Sierra
nine inches of rain San Bernadino County
where one & a half is usual
floods, slides

all is not usual

IT ALL HAS TO DO WITH THE ANIMAL—THE MEAT BLOOD
BONE & HAIR
IT'S ALL THERE—THE IMPACT

whether or not we touch—
I mean I don't have to touch you
to know you are there

"There is a weapon in the room"

TO KNOW
you only have to be there

groves of cedar, fir, oak—rock—running or standing
water—mountains, plains, river valleys—
snow & rain—the sun

you only have to be there

flowers opening in your head

I ain't the mother of any civilization

(the father of one girl-child—
but you have to start somewhere)

I don't know anything until I get there

"thin-chested?"

"WOLF MAN!"

I was always a gray wolf
like Pere Vidal of Old

looking after the chickens

save your silver bullets

I lope
in loops—circles
(miles & miles—but circles)
LE LOUP

like the "white bear"
sometimes a grizzly phenomenon

IF MY HEART IS WITH YOU
it is because you were here
with me
(I felt her heart
the pounding
in the ground
in the bottoms of my feet)

you know or you don't
it's like that
& you do or you don't
like that

settle in

how did you know?
my totem?

CANIS LUPIS
didn't know it showed

(23)

So early to wake—dark
& it has been a night of rain
I was surprised when the sun came—the rain gone
& like your gown, the camelias
fallen to the ground

the blackberries were not ripe
but we found two, nearly ready, not green
ate them

wrapped together, out of the wind
the gull put down over us, or so it seemed looking back
as we did, the side of the bluff, shale
rolling chunks & scree

the air was different

I was not to be found & you waited
found you, on the bed, the blanket, alone

we walked back, all
up hill, dust

he told me you were like a daughter to him

go easy, slow
I have a bad ankle

POEM FOR YELLOW HAIR

who did you come with, you asked
caw caw caw

           high in the trees
I think I was too drunk to answer

yellow light & all the greens
yellow
       after the rain
grass & willows
out my window
& the apple trees in blossom

maybe time to know each other

I don't know why I came
(not answering your question)

I followed the crows
(not answering your question)

on the beach
or in the mountains
maybe time
a few good moments

if you get to where you're going
                   (follow
the crows)
I'll be there

the horses fat from apples

BLUE GREEN A MOUNTAIN LAKE THE SKY
clear above

young red plum leaves, blossoms
snow on wet river stones

I came to you, you asked that I come
I wanted to, would have, come anyway

your tears, my tears

all day I listen to crows

the ground warm a warm rain

tears, the blue green a dress &
skin, wet river stones, tears

plum blossoms

crows, the sky

I hold you
someday you are going away

I'D CLIMB THE HIGHEST MOUNTAIN WITH YOU

if you thought you could make it

for Ed van Aelstyn

"SORRY LADY, THE TRAIN JUST LEFT 10 MINUTES AGO"
a long time going a long time gone

—a ticket to ride—

somebody stole my radio / I'm tuning in elsewhere
(the phonograph has a short in the arm)
a shot in the arm?
(the "H" train? "hard stuff"? NO! HARRIET!)

Venus Contaminated

the picture was of three wolves
a back shot, the ears, tipped, plainly visible
north of the Brooks Range—

I'm homesick, have never been there

with the advent of summer

the priest with his foot covering someone else's dropped
winning race ticket

travelers all

the secret: unequal portions, the balance in time
nothing comes apart in the same way
something always

on its way

just a question of what goes first

he'd told them not to go to Madrid—
Franco was still in power, but they went
& the night they were to arrive
he went to see a movie on the Spanish Civil War

(*29*)

the dead in the Basque country
the dead in Guernica
the dead in Madrid

TO DIE IN MADRID

three wolves

MUSSOLINI TOLD THEM THAT IF THEY WEREN'T
VICTORIOUS HE'D KILL THEM, HIS OWN
SOLDIERS

his wife says she was just a homebody

the sun today woke me
& later there was rain & wind
Snow—March 1st 1966—Westshore Drive, Belvedere
& on Mt. Tamalpais

the convict returned on his own
three nights alone in the Marin hills

they named the creeks after themselves
John & Bill Sochor
ALYESHKA, the Russians called it

contaminated, the Americans said
(they weren't—the Americans weren't—first)

it becomes a matter of selection, whether
you want it bad enough

(fighting wars is just a way out)

everything in unequal portions
mountains & valleys or
a little of everything: fish, fowl, meat

& don't forget the vegetables

brush with soft butter
SPRINKLE WITH SALT

* THE DOOR NEITHER OPEN NOR CLOSED *

& now Harriet
more demand than supply, he said

whether you want *what* bad enough??

marriage is an institution

three days in the Marin hills & he returned

IN UNEQUAL PROPORTIONS

take what you get give what you like

there ain't
no balance just
pulsation—wheels
they were

she wasn't making it with just anybody
she was making it with me

TO DIE ANYWHERE

like I said
home sick
I never been there

they just keep cutting out

If anything really wild happens, let me know.

IT HAPPENS ALL THE TIME.

*

VENUS IS A PLANET WHERE THE RUSSIANS STARTED LIFE TODAY

THERE ARE STILL THREE WOLVES NORTH OF THE BROOKS RANGE
 IN ALASKA, WHERE THE RUSSIANS ALSO SENT SHIPS

  & WHAT DID THE RUSSIANS HAVE TO DO WITH SPAIN,
                YOU ASK?

              *

it's been over an hour since that train left

I WENT TO SEE MY TRUE LOVE

at twelve, midnight, I started north
Stinson to Olema, twenty minutes
one deer before Bolinas

> Nobody's Child, dressed in black
> (Mary & Child, a postcard, behind her head)

> a bottle of vodka, can of V8
> didn't drink any

early evening, another night, same road
I saw half a dozen deer

> it was not an immaculate conception

blinking lights on the false front
jukebox music, laughter
drifting up the road
somebody twenty minutes in the phonebooth
before he walked, flashlight in his hand, up the hill

this is my scene * don't bug me * &c.

> it was very nice of you to come get this for her

> thoughtful kind brave clean & reverend

> what about cheerful

you're awful to do this for me

watched her dress, hair down, hair up, hair down
to the liquor store, deliver her
    to somebody else

on the first day I saw her
we knew

everybody did. All the others

    so where are you now???

    everybody

the thing to use, he said, is a shotgun
one shot—no report as from a rifle
a bow would be better

        we were shooting from the Packard at bottles

        I drove, he shot
        gallon bottles at 40 MPH he couldn't miss

        & that night a man killed shot with a shotgun
        the killer in a car fired on the move
        we had nothing to do with it, wondered
        had the killer practiced that afternoon

        maybe he knew he would hit his mark

Chicago everybody came from Chicago

    Nobody's Child

            she turned me into an elf delighted jumping
            the bell ringing ringing
            some strong man bringing down the sledge
            sending the weight
            again & again to the bell

    she's never been to a carnival

        no conception at all

the old man smiled at our holding hands

If he's such a bore, why do you sleep with him?

      *

were looking for a five-pointed star
found one with four, another with six
eucalyptus buttons, Golden Gate Park

       the cape was red velvet
             (what a big nose you have grandmother)

she rode into Stinson in a white Cadillac
angels fore & aft
       hell's angels leading the way
       the black & the white

           there was an old stove in the hotel
           we sat out back, sunshine & grass
           lilies & orange california poppies

she made friends with the coyotes, the wolves
       she never got to know
                   it was an experiment
       she left before the results were in

we were seated in the big chair

the quilt is the same color as those poppies

This is not the way I'd have done it.

if you had to be interrupted—
do it in style, Sam, making corn bread, Neal passing thru

the bottle fell, exploded
       pictures

watched squirrels, the park, Sacramento
hot, coffee on her raincoat coming home, the city cold

the donut shop, or over Sutro Baths, New Lucca

(Big John's?—were you dancing there the night I was there?)

amusement park pictures
out the window, near the tunnel, Broadway & Larkin
who found you???

                    there are horses tethered in the woods

      *

an earring, broken, hanging from the light string
        near your bed—I could reach it from the bed

the Dansk candle holder

one of the two long towels, thin stripes of blue & red,
        green, yellow & black, hung as curtain, to keep
        the late morning sun from the bed

the dresser, the drawers empty, the mirror—
        a nearly faded flower? painted to one side
        in green & red

        (I sat on the bed, watched you in the mirror
        as you brushed your hair, your chin up
        head back, then lowered—the final look
        before you turned)

the ice cream maker, a half empty bag of salt

these were the last of your things

two boxes of your old clothes sit in a corner
the house filled with strange people

I tried to write you a song

　　there was a swallow in May
　　a hummingbird a fuchsia

it was an ancient song
with no beginning nor end
　　like morning light
　　　medicine bells
　　　　bee stings

　　like broken glass & red beads

all the clocks were faces
　　set at ten-twenty

born at night / in red trimmed blue shoes

    out of the dark
  stars stars configurations
    fell in the gravel

Do you have your gun???

    (he had to back all the way out
    one-tenth mile down hill
    drove home alone—

    a messenger of the gods

    no mercury, nor packard, but a chevy)

she arrived for her birthday

I filled myself with rye
(it was a very special midnight)
let her shine on me

we were both born that night

(I wore my work shoes)

naked but for swimming suits we stood feet together
your feet between mine in the sand
you looked up at me gray eyes one small fleck of gold
palms sway the breeze warm from the sea
our bodies warm dark from the sun darker than our suits
in the darkness   there are stars over us   we kiss
up & down the beach figures move with the sea on the shore
a quiet splash of voices
it's all right you told me they can't see us

naked our bodies warm skin against skin
we made love in the grass your front yard
colored leaves orange & red yellow & brown blow up around us
leaves burn in the street smoke over us
children talk playing laughing
it's all right you told me it's only a dream

the mountain behind me, I drove south & west
passed three angels in Valley Ford
five more & a girl at the cross roads to Tomales
& four gassed up at Point Reyes Station, roared away
chrome & hair catching sunlight, to the north
to join the others

Billy & Toby were off, again
to Oregon, as per
I Ching, The Book of Changes

going thru changes

like music

harmoniously, minor discords
like she burned or threw away everything, always
burns her bridges
pulled the old light out of the ceiling
tore the wires loose, all connections

change gears

angels at every turn
all crossed roads

both sides, the streets lined with Harleys, choppers
of every description

> *he opened her coat*
> *& holding it open*
> *carefully & with expert eye*
> *examined*
> *what she had to offer*
> *so to speak, as it were*

a whole world

& nothing ever dies, it's all here
on every road, behind every tree
growing out of the ground, a beautiful
fire, flames

        I'm grinning

exhaust, carbon

        diamonds & threads
my mind is filled with diamonds & threads

we go off in all directions, thru intersections & crossed roads

a necklace to live in

SPARKES ROAD

California Poems / II

We change to keep all else the same

Crows fill the tree, get up
one by one, heavy, together
swing black across the blue
settle, one by one
together, fill the leafless tree

I burn six candles
white candles on a white plate

Six deer, dark in the snow, their heads
turned to me, & hawks
wheel above, blue sky
the deer do not move

Your hair has turned to Magpie feathers

Crossed & crossed the barbed stems
but the roses brush, brush
come together
                    one rose, rolls in the wind
petals layered, honey & dew
rolling rose
            & the glow

I was crawling around on the floor with her sister
when she came in, sat on the arm, the overstuffed chair
just so, her skirt adjusted, legs crossed
I have something for you, she said, held before her
two crystal balls, one clear, one ruby

Venus, pink, over the trees

                             apple blossoms
        dropping off
        you dreamed I sent you away

I lighted the lamp, smeared oil
on your breasts your thighs your stomach

the branches fill, leaves & green apples

Mars, opalescent orange, McIbbon's crystal ball
    reflects fire light
the sheen of ten brass shells whirring
she swings them over her very blond head

we dance as the moon disappears
howl & hoot dance drum
the orange moon disappears

she asks for a boy but I
bring none
she asks for a girl but I
only smile
                she writhes on her back
comes & comes
                hears us

we fuck in high oat grass
children in a circle around us

    "Here the world ends, here
  it begins. I fly between. Bring word
  after the beginning, before the end."

wide wings thru dark trees

all that he could catch of her was white light
        & the black behind

owl, just returned from the dead

        "I wasn't really there"

I crawled over the dark ground
planting squash, an owl
over my shoulder, the moon

she throws back her head, stretches
her arms hands, ripple of muscle
skin, the moon

clouds, shadows
between us
the ground mostly lighted

the flower first, fruit
full & rounded
the softest curve, ripple, moon

the laughter very soft

"I get crazy in the full moon"

the deer, out of the trees, downhill
the lake below, slowly, one foot
then another, down the dozed road

I had heard of her beauty

three hawks, low, crows below them
a calf, trying to stand
placenta still swinging from the cow

I caught her eyes

the owl, out of the trees
turns, returns
no place to come down

lightning, coming home
blue sky in the south
full moon moving
cloud to cloud, lakes lighted
dark hills behind darker hills
passed a horned owl, ruffled
one foot on his prey, deer &
two coyotes running

harder & harder to leave, she said

apples fall, the rooster crows
gray foggy summer dawn
apples in heavy dust

they stopped going south, the city
their boy swung on the rope
we drank what booze there was
filled their car, apples & pears

we came out of that city
like we meant to stay out
north across the bridge
thru Sausalito, & in Mill Valley
drank wine, ate Italian foods
Phoebe & McAdams turned back
we went on, the truck's bed
filled, the canopy
rattling & slapping
we stopped for all
wanting to go with us

from Tamalpais
we took the ridge road
sunset golden hills
red sky & blue
the Pacific, back of Bolinas

there were deer at the bottom
grazing the south edge
of that meadow

All through the night they rode
circled the Pole Star

blue white yellow & red ribbons
an iron bell before me

next to the cedar stood an oak
—the road ran between them—
I hung a rope from the oak, climbed it
could see more of the mountain—gold—in the north

the goat—Thunder—was killed at harvest
the dog ate her heart

we filled the room with hemp smoke—owl claws & feathers
outside, I looked into the dog's eyes
saw a dead man under the cedar

the blond woman came down from the mountains
watched over the child's birth

drunk, I pulled on a string of blue beads & iron bells
rung them—the bottom bell came off in my hand
I walked ahead, the road muddy in heavy rain
she followed, baby bundled in her arms
the wind louder than the rain where we came into the trees

where we'd watched for deer, along the river
the bell before me, a woman
crashed, killed herself
thrown from her car, her body under my truck

I found spotted mushrooms under the cedar

found a fox dead in the road—traded her skin
for the spotted feather of a golden eagle

with blue white yellow & red ribbons
I tied three sheep skulls high in the oak
at dusk with iron pots for drums
I sang a circle around the house & down the road

at midnight—the roar of a single motorcycle
then another & another—thirteen riders
beer to fill the bed of a truck
we sang, ran berserk, raced
all night over the dark hills—into & out of the flames
the best rider of them all fell into the coals
we pulled him out—unburned—put him to bed
he slept until dusk, was the last to leave

the child grew, one summer night squealed for joy
the iron pots rang where they hung
& the riders came again
burned their fire, all of the wood
in the morning one of them pierced the child's ears

when we left the place, he had returned
stood with others in the road, waved after us

rounding a curve, far to the east
a golden eagle flew up before us

Printed March 1971 in Santa Barbara
for the Black Sparrow Press by Noel Young.
Design by Barbara Martin. This edition
is limited to 800 copies in paper wrappers;
200 hardcover copies numbered & signed by
the poet; & 26 lettered presentation
copies handbound in boards by Earle Gray
& signed by the poet.

James Koller was born in 1936. He was raised in northern Illinois and left the midwest in 1959. For ten years he lived on the Pacific Coast (Washington, then California). The past year he has lived in Santa Fe, New Mexico.

His work has been anthologized in Europe, England, South America, and the United States. He is the author of five previous books of poetry. This book is his most extensive collection to date.

He is currently at work on his second novel.